Copyright © 2023

Title
Malala's Mission for the World

Written by
Aida Zaciragic

Illustrated by
Ana Grigorjev

ISBN (paperback) 978-91-527-8418-1
ISBN (hardback) 978-91-527-8420-4
ISBN (eBook) 978-91-527-8419-8

Publisher's Cataloging-in-Publication data
Names: Zaciragic, Aida, author. | Grigorjev, Ana, illustrator.
Title: Malala's mission for the world / written by Aida Zaciragic; illustrated by
Ana Grigorjev.
Description: Revised edition. | Västerås, Sweden: Aida Zaciragich, 2023. |
Summary: This book brings to life Malala's extraordinary story, teaching children
about the importance of education, bravery, and the belief that one person can
make a difference in the world.
Identifiers: ISBN: 978-91-527-8420-4 (hardcover) | 978-91-527-8418-1 (paperback)
| 978-91-527-8419-8 (ebook) Subjects: LCSH Yousafzai, Malala, 1997- --Juvenile
literature. | Girls--Education—Pakistan--Juvenile literature. | Sex discrimination
in education--Pakistan--Juvenile literature. | Women social reformers--Pakistan—
Biography--Juvenile literature. | BISAC BIOGRAPHY & AUTOBIOGRAPHY /
Women | BIOGRAPHY & AUTOBIOGRAPHY / Social Activists Classification:
LCC LC2330 .Y683 2023 | DDC 371.822095491--dc23

MALALA'S
MISSION FOR THE WORLD

Written by
AIDA ZACIRAGIC

Illustrated by
ANA GRIGORJEV

In a country called Pakistan, a little girl with hazel-brown eyes was born. Her parents named her Malala. She grew up with her father, a mother and two younger brothers.

Malala thought that she lived in the most beautiful place in the whole world. Their green valley was surrounded by high mountains, which were snow-covered even in the summer.

Through the valley flowed a fast river, Swat, green as the emerald. It was a fertile ground where a variety of fruits prospered such as plums, peaches and figs.

Malala's father was a teacher and at a very young age she attended his classes where she would listen to older pupils. She loved being among all of those children. She learned to read at a very young age. Before bedtime she loved sitting in her father's lap, listening to fairy- tales he used to read to her. She would look at him curiously with her big brown eyes and she couldn't fall asleep without hearing the end of the tale.

Malala was an unusual girl that stood out. She loved to read a lot and when she started going to school she wanted to be the best at everything. She won lots of awards that she kept on a shelf in her room. She had a lot of friends and they all loved her as much as she loved them.

When she got a little older she started noticing that people in her environment made a difference between boys and girls ... For instance, when a boy was born into some family there would be a huge celebration, and when a girl was born there would be no celebration.

But Malala's family was different. Her father and mother were very proud when they got a girl and they wanted to celebrate her birth. They gathered friends and relatives who put mint, dry fruits and candy in Malala's crib, just as they would do if it were a boy.

Malala's father, who was a teacher, opened a new school where both boys and girls could attend. In the beginning, not many children went to the school, but over time, the number of pupils grew, and it became a fairly large school. Malala had one best friend, and they were in the same class. The two of them spent a lot of time together from an early age. They would spend their days daydreaming and really enjoyed watching the Twilight saga together, pretending to be vampires, just like the characters in the movie.

Malala noticed that in her environment people made a difference between girls and boys. Boys could do pretty much anything, unlike girls. That made her angry and she thought it was unfair. She spent a lot of time thinking about it.

One night, while sitting at home watching TV, her mum asked her to throw out the garbage. There was a dump, not far from where they lived. Malala wasn't pleased because it was dark outside and the garbage smelled really bad.

When Malala came there, she saw a little girl among huge amount of garbage, about the same age as her. She could tell that the girl was very poor because her clothes were very dirty and old, and her hair was knotted.

She sorted the garbage and separated it into two different bags and not far from where she was standing she saw two boys doing the same. She wanted to go up to them and talk to them but she didn't dare to do so, because it was really dark.

When she got home she told her dad what she saw. She begged him to go there and talk to them. She told him: "Daddy, please, can they come to our school too?" When they got to that place, there was nobody around.

In Malala's country you had to pay to go to school and a lot of those children did not go to school. Since their parents were poor they could not afford to pay to go to school.

Some of the children didn't even have parents and they were forced to get by on their own. That made Malala sad and she would often think about it.

She dreamt about being able to help them.

Then came the terrible events that changed everything in Malala's life. She overheard grownups talking about a possible war. They were shocked and afraid when groups of strange, armed men came to their peaceful valley. These people—called the Taliban—started interfering in people's lives, telling them what they could do and what they were no longer allowed to do. No one could oppose them because there were so many Taliban, and they had weapons. People were afraid to even leave their homes.

The Taliban did not want the people in the valley to be free—especially the women and children. According to the Taliban laws, people were no longer allowed to watch TV. But worst of all, girls were no longer allowed to go to school.

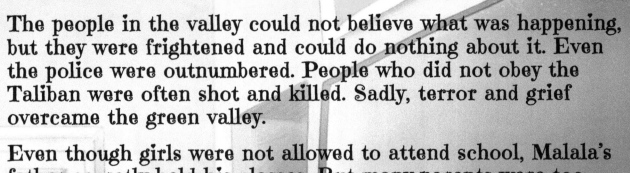

The people in the valley could not believe what was happening, but they were frightened and could do nothing about it. Even the police were outnumbered. People who did not obey the Taliban were often shot and killed. Sadly, terror and grief overcame the green valley.

Even though girls were not allowed to attend school, Malala's father secretly held his classes. But many parents were too worried, so only a few children still came to school.

The world was informed about what was going on in Malala's valley. One day, a TV journalist asked Malala's father if he knew any girl who would keep a journal and go on TV to tell the world about the ongoing events. "Why not me?" asked Malala. "I've never kept a journal before, but I want to try. I want the world to know what is going on here. Girls have the right to education! No one can take it from us!"

Malala became a voice. Everyone listened.

Malala's father became worried about the dangers of the Taliban. Instead of using her real name, Malala was to be called "Gul Makai." The journalist asked her about her life, how she spent her days, what she did with her friends, and if she had any dreams. He told her about a girl named Anne Frank who kept a journal during World War 2 and became known worldwide.

Malala told the journalist that she was still going to school secretly, and nothing could change her mind. It was dangerous to go on the air, but Malala thought that since she was just a child, the Taliban would not harm her. The program was aired in most parts of the world.

"Gul Makai's" journal became known everywhere. People were extremely interested in what was happening.

When the world learned that "Gul Makai" was really Malala, she received many awards for her courage and dedication. Malala said, "I don't want to stop learning. If girls can't go to school, we will educate ourselves!"

Despite everything, it became public that Gul was really Malala. She received many awards for her courage and dedication.

Then...one sunny day, something horrible happened when Malala was returning home from school. Suddenly, as the children were talking and laughing, the bus was stopped by two unknown men who entered the bus. "Who is Malala?" they demanded. Thinking they were journalists wanting to interview her, a few of the children looked over at Malala.

All of a sudden, shots were fired in her direction.

The men ran away. Children cried. How were they to have known that the men were Taliban? Malala and two other girls were wounded and were transferred by ambulance to a hospital. Malala's injuries were the most serious because one of the shots had hit her head, The other girls were soon released from the hospital, but Malala remained unconscious.

No one knew if she would live. The whole world was concerned, as people everywhere prayed for the brave girl to be well. The other girls were soon released from the hospital, but Malala remained unconscious.

Doctors in her country did everything they possibly could. They decided to transfer her to Great Britain for further treatment. Her condition was unstable because she didn't wake up.

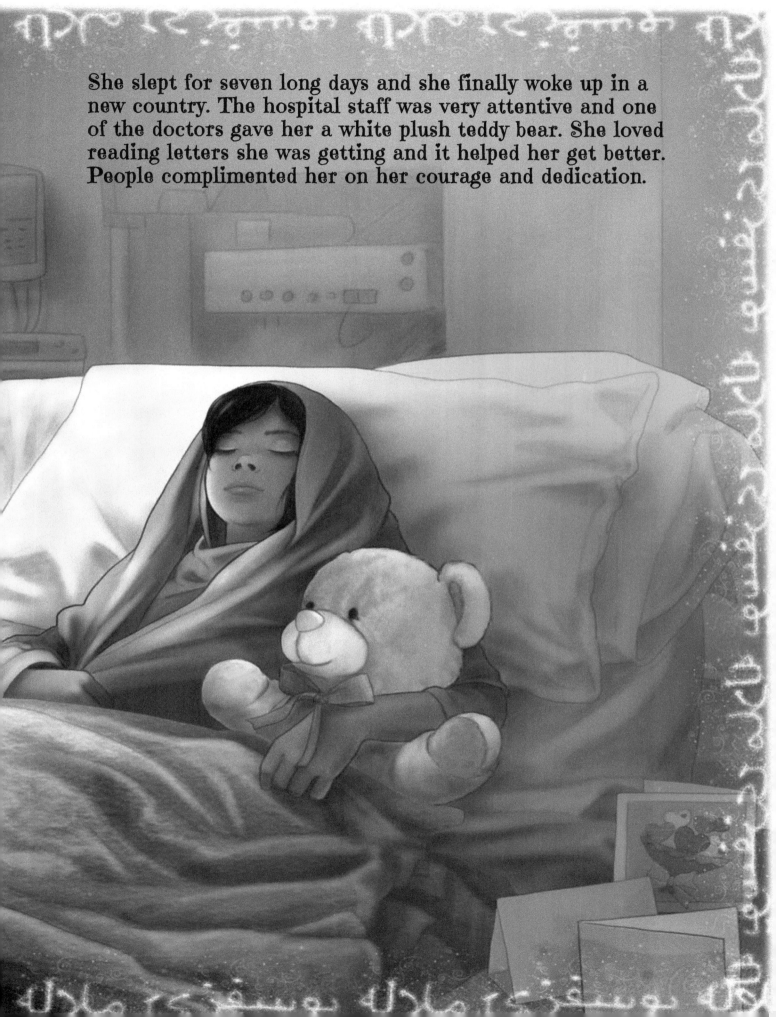

She slept for seven long days and she finally woke up in a new country. The hospital staff was very attentive and one of the doctors gave her a white plush teddy bear. She loved reading letters she was getting and it helped her get better. People complimented her on her courage and dedication.

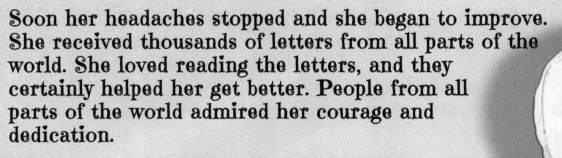

Soon her headaches stopped and she began to improve. She received thousands of letters from all parts of the world. She loved reading the letters, and they certainly helped her get better. People from all parts of the world admired her courage and dedication.

The hospital staff treated her with kindness, but she missed her family very much. She often spoke to them over the phone. Some time later Malala's family came and they were reunited.

Malala was soon released from the hospital and they all moved into an apartment where they continued living happily together.Her courage became well known to the whole world.

She was nominated for the Nobel Peace Prize. It was the first time that a child was nominated for this award.

The Nobel Prize is the most prestigious award and it is given annually for peace, science and literature.

Malala continued with her life, in a new country. She started going to school and made a lot of new friends there. Still, she missed her country. She really loved her country, a beautiful green valley, and, most of all, she missed her good friends.

Today, people in the whole world know who Malala is. The girl fighting for young girls' right to education; equal rights for boys and girls. The bravest girl in the world. Despite everything that happened to her, Malala has been fighting for all children that live in poverty in other countries and she is dedicated to helping them.

In some parts of the world, girls are still not allowed to go to school.

It is now Malala's time to do everything she used to dream about; to change the destiny of many struggling children, in all parts of the world.

ABOUT THE AUTHOR

Aida Zaciragic embarked on an amazing journey as she went from being a school teacher to becoming an award-winning author. Her fascination with life, spanning her past, present, and future, is beautifully portrayed in her stories.

Although Aida has been residing in Sweden for the past 30 years, her roots trace back to Bosnia and Herzegovina, lands once inhabited by kings. As a child, the stories she heard about these kings fueled her imagination. She is the author of The Kingdom of White Lilies, which is regarded as a cherished treasure in Bosnian literature. Her second book, The Law of Freedom, earned her an award at the Sarajevo Book Fair in 2010.

ARE YOU FEELING EMPOWERED TO HELP SAVE THE WORLD?

Help us spread the word of Malala's incredible mission to empower young women with the same educational rights and freedom as men.

Please consider leaving a review on Amazon to encourage others to read this book and support the mission. Scan the QR code above to leave a review.

HER CONFIDENCE.

HER DRAW TO
SOCIAL ACTIVISM.

HER PASSION
FOR LEADERSHIP.

HER FUTURE STARTS TODAY.

Thank You

FOR YOUR ORDER

I hope you'll join me for more.

As parents, we play a crucial role in nurturing our children's self-confidence and instilling in them a sense of social justice and equality for all.

It's important to empower our girls to be strong, compassionate individuals who believe in themselves and in creating a fair and just world.

Ready to kick-start your journey? Subscribe here:

https://aidazaciragic.com

Printed in the USA
CPSIA information can be obtained
at www.ICGtesting.com
LVHW061253211123
764112LV00014B/701

9 789152 784204